This is NOT for you!

Jennifer Zak

Presentation by *BookLeaf Publishing*

Web: www.bookleafpub.com

E-mail: info@bookleafpub.com

ISBN: 978-93-95784-18-4

First edition 2022

DEDICATION

To anyone lucky enough to have played my temporary muse. You're Welcome!

PREFACE

This is not for you is exactly that. I added "getting a book published" to my bucket list when I was in 9th grade. This was finally done for me to share my craft with anyone appreciative. This is raw passion of moments that made me feel some sort of way. Good, bad and ugly truths that often people just brush under a rug. I choose to use my words to explain how I feel. This released me mentally and emotionally from many things. If you personally know me you may read through and find things that pertain to you. Know I will never apologize for the way someone made me feel. If you don't like it perhaps you will reflect on what you did to cause such emotion. Putting these poems into peoples hands sent me through fear and self doubt like no other. I hope you find at least one that you will read over and over. If you relate to any of these pieces I hope my words help you explain to someone what you have not been able to say. I have come to accept that I am the girl in the corner who is a mute but full of emotion. Attached is from a page poet.

Unicorn

I'll have you thinking this can't be real
She's not legit
Let's red flag categorize her shit
She's gotta be playing with me

This hookup culture has turned you cold
Not knowing what to do with something
authentic
Do you dare believe in unicorns and aliens
Or does this girl just not exist anymore

I only give the best pieces of me if I'm feeling
you
Everyone else gets that Halloween version of me
Your access to me is undenied
While others get that social media me

You may think it's too good to be true
Then I'll become the 1 that got away
The 1 you remember when ur back in the muck
of these women today

If only you let yourself realize I am a genuine
one
No representative
but that shit you dream of type one

Love all in your face
Cuddle you to death type of factual one

You either accept it and fall down my rabbit hole
Or you can reject it
Be scared of it
Can't trust it
And get that regret in your gut when you see
someone else with it

I'm not for the weak at heart
As not everyone can properly handle this
A bonafide love of your life
Have you on your knees weak
But standing up to the world with this woman at
your back

Have you unfuckwithable
Cuz nobody can knock a man down who feels
20 feet tall
With this extremely rare female by your side
nothing is impossible

Build you up
To be my world
My future
My strength
But my weakness all at the same time
This love is the historical kind

Imposter

I heard you stole my words
Rewrote them to fit her

You can have them
In hopes you get some clarity

Clarity in the fact that you can't forget me
You want to be like me
Treat someone with the love I gave you
Imposter me
to win HER over

You would never have my sincerity though
As you don't know how to live
honestly
You run off lies & bullshit
Probably have 2 or 3 sneaky links

Manipulate and corrupt her
Reflect my ways upon her
Probably double dealing behind her
You don't deserve her

Swindling your way into hearts
To then do as you please
End up turning them into pieces of pain
Simply because you live like a thief

So take my words I gave to you
Imitate my love language
Thieve my ways and hook 'em
Suffer the consequences of your larceny

As you lay there inside of her trying to have
what you lost
Trying to fill a void
Take your copycat ways and drown between her
thighs
Make sure that's where you hide your tears so
she thinks ur doing a good job

Let him in

I was thrown off & ...sucked in by the vibe
That fucking FEELING of being alive

He instantly sparked that shit but with what
intent
Now I gotta stop asking when we gonna slide

I gotta back off & dim this life
This life I let die before it was smacked back
alive
It's gotta go back to sleep
It's gotta die

I feel the fool for letting him in
Bringing back that
KUNTY.
RUSSIAN.
BARBIE Jen

This mind is too much, this heart is too big
I'm putting it back to beat quietly instead

When I say I let him in
I mean I let him INNNN
And I can still feel him

Knowing he wasn't safe to let into this brain
I should have left it at the DM

FUCK!!!!! but that smile drew me in
That genuine good soul vibe
We just clicked the same

Now I feel I should flip it off
Throw myself to the friend zone
That spot I thrive

He's not as described or perhaps just
pre-occupied
Either way
I would have gave him life
Gave him that KING status
But I fall off to the side
Along with my applied pressure & effort

I thought fate finally woke up and shined
But that bitch must HATE my life!!!!

I don't want to bother the man's peace
I just wanted to feed its supply

Back off woman
He's just not feeling your vibe
If only I could stop that postman with that letter
Wasted message delivered
Fuck u Apple - pleeeease Activate that unsend

The things he says over the phone

With a voice so perfect
Instantly makes me wet
Just the thought of it alters my mood

I want him so many times a day
To hear him say "Right there"
And "that's the spot"
While he grabs my hips to hold me there

This devil dick got me to orgasm like no other
He is trouble in a whole different form
I want to please him on repeat
Thank God he lives a distance away

I would wake him up and put him to sleep
Have him living between these thighs
Sending me through my day wet
And him drained on E til we reconnect

To feel his hands on me
Kissing his perfectly soft lips
To smell his scent mixed with mine
Just to hear the control in his words

I want this man for myself
I feel we blend so well
I can't have him when I want but I'll wait for
him
Wait until I can feel his arms around me

He makes me feel safe
Makes me want to be open to loving
Loving him and what he brings
But right now I just want him badly.

When I have you

When I have you..
It may not be today
or next week
But when I do
I want you to remember this night.

When I drop hints
that I want your hands on me
Your skin touching mine
The scent of your cologne left in my hair

When I send you pics
of the parts of my body
I am yearning for your hands to touch
Even for you to tease

When I am dreaming of you
And all of the places I want to kiss
To run my hands over your soft skin
to feel your reaction to me

When I finally have you
will it be the end of me
I'm feeling you in other ways

ways I didn't want to
Kinda wish you kept on walking

When I have these thoguhts about you
do you think I'm crazy
Can you see how I look at you
As I passionately look you over

When I imagine it
I swear it woud be worth it
So why so hesitant
that is the question
I want it

When I am no longer afraid
to feel someone new
As I am not an empty soul
Nor a tinder date

When I hear your voice
it gives me goosebumps
Especially the way you say Jennifer!
I pray that you talk dirty to me

When I have you
This is what you said to me
The first night we met
You already knew how this would end

Will I remember it
Will I replay it in my head
As I do the moment we met
or will my high expectation
For amazing be the death of it

when I finally have you
I will be able to breathe
Calm the fidgeting
stop the wondering

When I finally have you
will I regret it
when I finally have you
will I melt onto your chest after
and wish I never stopped for you

When I finally have you
Will it be awkward
When I finally have you
Feeling you agaisnt me,in me
will I run

When I met you
I found my smile again
So if I have you
Will I lose my sanity
and wish i never met you

Racing Mind

As I sit with nervous energy
He tempts me
Walking out in only a towel
Millions of thoughts run through my mind

Would if I am behind you
Rubbing your back
I feel my mood switch
and tell you to

put your hands
on the table.

My voice is
lower
slower

Hands.
Table.
Now.

You look up at me
Smirk
Slowly place your hands in position

I move quickly
Your smirk becomes surprise
Then sneer
Then grimace
and your hands move instinctively
to protect you from me

I sigh
disappointed in your disobedience
I reach around
Grab delicate parts of you
And I speak again
Slowly
Against your ear

Put.
Your.
Fucking.
Hands.
On.
The
FUCKING.
Table.

You move a bit faster
Then hesitate
Hovering your hands before submitting

I take my time

Kissing
Biting
Touching
Watching

Every flinch makes me wetter
Every sound makes me hotter

I circle you
Face you
I go for your throat and watch
as you struggle for stillness
 I linger
Just a bit beyond the space between
Fear & panic then excitement

The look on your face
makes me want to fuck you
so I straddle you
run my tongue around the edges
of your perfect lips feeling the softness
Biting.
and whisper

"You're lucky"

You'd be a beautiful mess
Before I was done with you.

you look at me and hold my gaze
I see the shift in your eyes
As your hands leave the table
then wrap around my hair

You tighten your grip
Bend me as my breath catches
And you smile
The moment I realize my turn is over.

If I had a gun to your head

Love never ends well
If it's not til death it's til betrayed
you lied to keep from getting hurt
With no regard to the damage you caused me
So please realize who put us here

You're standing in front of me
Begging me to allow your lungs more breath
and that rotten heart more beats
But I desire to save all women from your
fuckery

The 1st bullet to your knee
As you said you couldn't wait to drop down in
front of me
Wanted me as your wife for life
Claiming that no-one else would suffice

I will send a bullet straight for your mouth
The mouth that spued all your lies
That fucking mouth sucked my soul from my
body every time you had to apologize
The mouth that spit venom disguised as love
That mouth that took 24 years of my life

That God damn amazing mouth that lived
between these thighs

Do I dare waste a bullet on that weak ass dick
It presents as half dead as is
You used to be so young and eager now just old
and used up like the neighborhood whore
We'll exchange that hormone shot for bullet #3
There is no need for further sexual interaction

The last bullet is straight to the head
Allow me to bring your life to an end
I am no God just a demon you created
I will finally calm that PTSD mind
And relieve you of your tormented ego
This is a judgement you have earned and I'm
happy to deliver.

Only husbands need apply

I've had a few come through
Do what they were supposed to
Threw a ring on it
All for me to throw it back
So many people make you fall
Fall for a representative of themselves
Someone they wish they could be
But never match their own identity
You can keep those damaged beyond repair...
Those I'll do what I want whenever boys
My worst trait is doing girlfriend shit for a hello
beautiful
And doing wife shit for a man who isn't ready.
The struggle is real for a lovergirl
In this world full of tinder and hinge
Bumble and plenty of fish
When all I want is rock steady 90s R&B
love y'all don't know about
I don't need wine & dined
I need cuddles, love and time
I need you to appreciate my vibe
Love me back like you need me in your life
I don't want to kick you out in the morning

I want to lay on top of you until it's breakfast in
bed
Sleep, Eat, Sex and repeat
Those cute little couple pics
then grown and sexy dinner dates
Be there for me on those shitty days
We can catch flights and escape the stress.
If you can make me smile I may just fall in love
Please be prepared to catch this chick
Instead of a fuckboy who keeps fumbling this
shit

False Advertisement

My brain tells me to walk away
Because my heart does too much
I don't know how to be fake
Which is why I'm so acquainted with heartbreak
See the best in someone that they don't see
themselves
Why does he think I'll do him as she did
This the GOAT baby
There is no fumbling here
You're always dropping the ball though
Then pull me back in with a phone call
I listened to what you said you wanted
But you toss my effort like it's given easily
You don't know my pains & growth
I've been where you are
Unfortunate for you your fumbling hard
You'll realize it when it's too late
Maybe try and come back this way
Things have calmed down you'll say
But I may not be around your way
Why did I bother
Tried to make you feel wanted and loved
But it just was not my place
To give you what you lost

Or perhaps never had.
Being alone is amazing
but imagine being treated like you're everything
Now it is not my concern.
I'll sit by and watch from afar
see who you select to place in the job I had
applied for

To lose a family member who still breathes

As these pics & memories pop up with no ease
One would not believe we used to be thick as
thieves
How you turn your back on sisters who always
had yours
Conniving & menacing words wishing death on
us
Backstabbing moves in secret to even unfriend
us
Stealing our relationship with your kin
Leaving us out of his life like an unknown
sibling
You have grown up to think you are a King
But we have no need to bow down to you like
your chosen "Queen"
You choose to be amongst the snakes in this
grass
Perhaps because that's where you now fit in
Lies upon lies and disrespect fed
I hope one day you see that ghetto trash was a
downfall
not a step up instead
I used to call you my best friend
Now ur just a living lost brother instead.

Intimidating

So I hear I intimidate you
Not just you but many
This big dick energy is only allowed by men
I will not apologize for my demeanor
Simply because of your fear to redeem her
Is it my big girl career
Or this bold attitude I hold
I used to be a fighter
Now I'm the lover instead
Are you afraid you cannot handle it
Or fear the fact you cannot mistreat it
Boss me around?
Allow me to be the submissive if your strong
enough
Intimidated by my sounds
But constantly say I'm beautiful
I do not bite
Unless your the deserving kind
Find your big boy pants
Learn to use your words
and find yourself the envied one
As you stand next to this girl

If I Could Write

If I could write something beautiful that
surpasses beautiful
for you
It would be to tell you that to me
you've never lost a place in my heart
It would be to say that upon hearing your voice
my heart jumped a little and settled once again
in the comfort of our space.
If I could write something beautiful
there would be the scent of roses
and the lit candle in the corner of our room.
I would tell you how my soul just rested calmly
in your company...
I would tell you that not a thing about you has
changed for me
except the changes that needed be
and they don't impact the you I see.
I embrace all you are and all you've come to be.

If I could write something beautiful for you
there would be music that you love
and the safety of a warm and tender hug
all wrapped in words that words could never say,
except how glad I am to have known you then
and to cherish our memories today.

For My Sister

I fear I will crack one day
And let you see how this breaks my heart in so
many ways
Always putting on a strong front
Only to try and match your positive one
If I were you I sure would not be living
Your courage and mindset is aspiring
You sit there in a Groundhog Day life
While your own family doesn't come by
Not your sons nor their girlfriends
Your sisters or your brother
Not an Aunt or an Uncle
Or a cousin either.
Would if they sat there alone
Unable to do for themselves
Would you have been there for them in the same
way
I fly 1300 miles to sit with you for a couple
hours
Feeling I can do nothing to fix your life
Wishing I could give my life for you to survive
This life is not fair
The way it takes and leaves us in despair
The emotional toll your situation takes on me I
try not to share

Often times it is not easy to bear
I grew up wanting to be like you
For you to now say you live vicariously through
me
From Let's go crazy to I would die for you
This life is so fucking uneasy
But we try to still party like it's 1999
Thoughts of you give me enormous anxiety
But with you I do my best to show laid back and
comedy
with no hope of you getting better soon
If I do not have you who do I talk to
One other sister to lean on who I have to fear for
Will I lose you to then take care of her
Is being a sister just dreading that purple rain
When the little sister has to play big sister
This life is always setting us up for a fall
Just remember Baby you're a star!

Another Life

I am over you
Since the moment you spit in my face
Sad thing is
I would have forgave the physicalities
As I often forgave your Kanye profanities
You took full advantage of my love
Played my daughter with your fake father bluff
In more than our hearts you left a hole
Your pictures are trashed and things burned
Unfortunately in my mind your soul has lived
and now I had to kill it
cover it with the poison you exuded
I thought we were pure love
but you truly were Satan in human form
No care what you do to others
as long as your woe is me is having its cake and
eating it too
As much as I wish you would rot in your
dreadful life
that does not serve me or my soul
I know you think of me
I know at times you miss me
I know you remember how I felt
So I will move forward healed

and one day loved by someone in ways you wish
you could
Ways you tried and failed
It does not matter who you end up with
I will pray for her safety in every aspect
I know you and whoever
will never be you and I
She will never do as I did
You will die regretting what you did
you will die missing me
You will die thinking of our crazy love
and you will still yearn for me
Until that last breath and beyond
But please do me the favor
and don't find me in that next life

He is mad

He is mad
He is rushing
to her
from her
by her
in her
for her
it's always her
He cannot stop
she keeps him
high
low
in
out
up and down
spinning
around
He loves her
madly
foolishly
carelessly
wrecklessly
tirelessly
He wants her
sefishly

jealously
covetously
endlessly
only

She

a flood of sexual power
she's bigger than the sky
she's higher than the moon
she's harder than a diamond
and she's worth a million too
she never will come down
she never will go back
she'll never accept anything
less than everything and then
she still desires more
she craves to get much higher
she wills to grow a million fold
and set the world on fire
she never will accept
she never will conform
to pass through life anonymous
in an uninspired world.

Beware

You have entered
the forbidden caverns of my mind,
secretly stepping into my soul
like a ghost through a wall
But beware,
for the dreams within my mind
may consume you
if you look too far into them.
I am nothing that I seem.
I am a walking, talking, living, breathing
open wound that may never heal;
possibly devouring you as well
if you overstay your welcome.
You must escape me before its too late.
I've never held onto anything sacred
for my mind is haunted and tormented.
Some people call it a gift or a craft
but these dreams do nothing other than taunt my
ass.
I lie awake, avoiding the morning light.
I'm all alone, another sleepless night.
I sit with shades drawn as the hours pass,
wondering how long these nightmares will last.
When I dare to sleep, they enter my dreams.
I'm under their hypnotic trance it seems.

Each time I close my eyes, I am pulled from this world
I journey to the place where the shattered ones walk,
where the silent spirits watch, and the lost souls talk.
I hear the voices echo from beyond the darkness,
the most menacing sounds rising from the black abyss.
The words spoken penetrate deep into my soul.
I don't know what's happening, I'm losing control.
A ghostly sensation moves throughout my body
as I feel the fear rising up from inside me.
The voices, I hear them from all possible directions,
the coldness running through my veins like a lethal injection.
So now at night I stay awake to guard myself from them,
hidden in the shadows to keep them from destroying my soul too.
In the darkness I sit alone and wait for them to strike,
not knowing where they are, or what their new form looks like.
I know living my life in fear is not the best thing to do
but its better than letting myself be taken by you.

Hypnotized

My eyes. My stare. My mouth. My lips. My heart.
My sounds. My touch. My skin. My body. My soul.
Hynotized under your spell.
A wicked and fascinating spell which controls
every part of me. Of my life. My heart and soul.
You leave me feeling weak, out of breath and
powerless.
I live for your breath. I crave your skin.
I think only thoughts of you.
24 hours aren't enough hours in the day to be with
you.
The distance eternal. The nights endless.
The days empty without you in them. You control
me.
I speak, I breathe, I feel, I am only if you request it
so.
Strong damn spell ehich I could never fall out of.
Twisted and engraved in every cell of my being is
your name,
your flavor, your smell, your blood, your sweat.
Over and over again I hear your life echo in me.
Over and over again I hear me echo
the sounds of passion, sex, lust and desire.
All loud. All embraced. All engaged. All of me.
Hypnotized by you

Hypocrite

Hypocrite, Hypocrite
From where did you come
Pick and choose the bricks in my wall
Pile them high one by one

Hypocrite, hypocrite
Such a flamboyant display

With the up most indignation
You carry on this way

Hypocrite, Hypocrite
Declare your judgmental decrees

Pick and decide
What only pertains to me

Hypocrite, Hypocrite
Carefully state your venom on this fine day

This bitch will not tolerate
Hurtful words you have to say

Hypocrite, Hypocrite
In the end you will lose

When you bend over backwards
To shit out the harmful words you choose

Passion

I see you holding me close to you,
Squeezing my body tight.
But for all I see as I daydream-
I know I'll get tenfold tonight.

Running your palms across my breast,
As I tremble and bite my lip.
Feeling your hands upon my chest,
The softness of each fingertip.

Tasting my neck so sweet, so soft,
And slowly lowering your kiss.
Over my navel, across my thighs,
And finally into pure bliss.

Looking upon my face from below-
As I tilt back my head.
Feeling fountains begin to flow-
As I ease back on the bed.

My "innocent little devil" look-
Crying insatiably with the sensation.
Lip to lip lapping up every drip-
From the well of my creation.

The way I pull you up by your hair-
To the heat of my mouth, on fire.
No other thoughts, no other cares,
Just the quenching of mad desire.

Riding the tide of passion,
Pushing your way into me.
On the waves of my emotion-
In slow motion, so sweet and true.

Pulse pounding in resounding rapture,
Taken to the hilt, then just past.
Rhythm growing, faces glowing,
The climax coming fast.

That heated, illicit look-
Of ecstasy across your eyes.
The culmination nearing-
Within my undulating thighs.
Echoing throughout the room-
On overindulgent cries.

The sultry look upon your face-
In reaching that gyrating gush.
The way I bite your fingers-
When you try to make me hush.

My arching back, my fingernails,
My perfume mixed with sweat.
The way you keep rubbing against me-
With your desires leaving you so content.

The way when your beat dead and ready-
To fall face first to the floor,
I put my sweet lips to your ear-
And whisper, "I want more! "

Because of Me

My words will bring to life the deepest part of
your untouched soul
My emotions will pull you in and force you to
feel
My raw passion will bring yours to the surface
with me, you will not be able to ignore who you
were meant to be
as I force you to face your fears
and teach you about the darkness of your needs

I will overload you
I will infect you
I will be your newest addiction
I will become your motivation to create
I will effortlessly bring you to your knees
I will teach you how to let go

Your body willl ache for me
Your heart will break for me
You will become drenched in lust
You will become a slave to my body
You will need a different kind of release
Because of me

My intensity is undeniable
My beauty is unmistakable
My honesty is refreshing
My darkness is seductive
My words are powerful
My imagination is boundless

The more you know me the more you will learn
about yourself
I'll bring out the darkest parts
I'll expose every weakness
and you willl embrace me
Unable to deny the connection
Because of me

* 9 7 8 9 3 9 5 7 8 4 1 8 4 *